The Call of the Kokako

Poems from far-flung places

Anthony Boniface

BRAMBLEBY BOOKS

ISBN 9781908241054
eISBN 9781908241108

Published 2011 by
Brambleby Books Ltd., UK
www.bramblebybooks.co.uk

Cover design by Creatix Design
'The Kokako pair' drawing is by the
New Zealand artist Sam Clark

Printed and bound by Printondemand-worldwide, UK
FSC and PFSC accredited

The Call of the Kokako

This book is dedicated to my family and friends and to all those pupils and students whom I taught and who shared my love and interest in plants, animals, microbes and molecules, whose study makes life worthwhile.

About the author

Anthony Boniface was born in London in 1936. Although living in a North London suburb, he developed a keen interest in natural history. He began writing poetry in the sixth form continuing at university where he studied Botany at Kings College, London and Microbiology at University College, London. During a career in school teaching, poetry writing lapsed resuming after retirement. Inspiration came mainly from holidays spent bird watching and plant hunting around the world with his wife. He gained several awards for poems entered in local poetry competitions and has had two poems published in a literary magazine.

Contents

Queensland Rainforest

Green Catbird in the canopy.
Dark Whipbird tossing leaves.
A Yellow Robin watching me
Between the Booyong trees.

Satin Bowerbird builds a bower.
He decorates in blue,
Collecting feathers and blue flowers
To please a female's view.

Brush-turkey scrapes the litter round;
He builds a warm abode.
His female lays eggs in the mound
Like other megapodes.

Now Rufous Fantail waves his tail
Close to the forest floor.
Defence of nest-site by the male
Accounts for what I saw.

Black iridescent riflebird
Rasps through the morning light.
Detection of this call once heard
Reveals a startling sight.

Just Darwinian selection
Has shaped each forest bird.
Without need for God's creation,
Evolution has occurred.

Flame Trees

Flame trees in the forest
Spot-lighting the landscape,
Illuminating life.

In the drought
I shed my leaves.
Shall I flower too
In contrast with black branches?
Burn in the darkness;
Show pathways of success
To those I teach,
Or maybe kindle greater minds than mine
To look, and understand
The living things that many just ignore
Or worse, kill casually.

In my perpetual quest
To find acceptance
Could I ignite a forest fire
As peaceful as this flaming tree
Before the petals fall?

Lesson in Evolution

The Laughing Kookaburra
Has a voice which is well-known.
Invertebrates and reptiles
The food preference they've shown,
Unlike other kingfishers
All of which they have outgrown.
Monogamy's their lifestyle
But the young aren't left alone;
Their brothers and their sisters
Independence they postpone
And help their parents feed them
Till the family has flown.
Their genes are really selfish;
Now the sceptics must atone.

Australian Ecosystem

Brown Honeyeaters pollinate,
Flash forest fires help germinate,
These Banksias illuminate
How species can cooperate
In ways that truly fascinate,
And help the teachers educate
The children to appreciate
How each of them associates
With others that reciprocate
Until some humans devastate
Without the sense to hesitate;
Discuss the problem and debate
How to sustain a stable state.
If only we could calculate
The best way we should operate
So that we all could integrate
Before it really is too late.

The Wandering Albatross

Delight at the sight
Of these lovely birds
Squabbling with the Giant Petrels
Over the food
Tied to the back of the boat,
Rolling gently in the swell,
At this point
Where our paths crossed.

They had glided
Close to the water,
Whilst we had jetted towards them,
Chaperoned by Cape Pigeons,
To watch and listen,
Sharing their lonely lives
For a fraction of the time
They spent climbing the waves.

Then they flew
From our rendezvous,
Whilst we jetted away
From this wonderful morning,
Enhanced forever in the future
By a memory
Of these ocean wanderers,
With their wings outstretched,
Intimidating their rivals …
And leaving us
In eternal admiration
Of these avian angels
That we had travelled
So far around the world
To see.

Kiwis probing the Sand

The waves crashed on the beach
Swishing over the sand,
Whilst on the high tide line
The Kiwis probed the kelp
Searching for sand hoppers
On which to feed.

But years before, man's minion, rat
Had walked the mooring ropes
To kill these flightless birds,
Who failed to understand
That they themselves were food.

But rat forgot his cunning
And did not sense the poison
That later men had set
To punish him.

Now we repay the debt,
The promise has been kept,
And whilst most people slept,
We through the forest crept,
To watch these birds.

Tonight we wish to thank
New Zealander's we met,
Who led us to this shore
So we could evermore
Recall the birds we saw,
Knowing so many care
That Kiwis are still there
Probing the sand.

The Takahe

Takahe from Tiritiri
Stalked his island lair,
Determining at lunch time
If anyone was there.

He sampled picnic sandwiches
And stole the ripest fruit,
But when our meal was eaten
He nibbled at our boots.

Takahe from Tiritiri
Possessed a scarlet beak.
He sidled up on his red feet
And gave our legs a tweak.

He ran along the pathways
Intercepting the unwary:
He chased them to the jetty
If they treated him unfairly.

Takahe from Tiritiri
Should have known better.
His appetite for bits of bread
Would his life endanger.

So if you visit Tiritiri
Keep your lunch secured,
And make sure that the Takahe's
Existence is assured.

New Year Resolution

Fiordland Crested Penguins ride the surf,
Attempting to maintain an upright stance
Before they are dragged back into the waves,
Sucked into turmoil by the undertow,
Until they try again to reach their young
And walk with proud achievement up the beach.

Whilst I, remember, on this New Year's Day,
Decide I could these penguins emulate,
Resolve to live in their determined way
And march towards a new environment.
But we aren't programmed to achieve our dreams.
We crystallize in patterns that depend
On ways our simple atoms interact
To build the crystal lattice of our lives,
Making decisions that can change the path,
Yet reach the same inevitable end.

The Secret

The tree branches flow.
The silent winds blow.
A stream of cloud scuds
Above glistening snow.
Far in the distance,
No hope of assistance,
A van with a secret
That no one will know.

African Holiday

The sky shone brilliant black,
And silver stars now track
Their path within the Milky Way;
Our footsteps scrunch through dusty sand,
And nebulae of torchlight
Guide our feet.
Our laughter warms the darkness,
Awakening the memory of orange flowers,
Firing the landscape,
Dancing in the breath of Africa,
As they open to the gentle passion of the sun.
Moist kisses soon impatiently unlock
Our purring pleasure amongst rounded rocks;
And distant water roars within our ears,
Reminding us of passion in the past,
Rekindling our love in later years.

Ostrich

They call me altruistic
But I'm selfish just the same,
I laid my eggs together
When another female came,
She added her own ova
So I cannot take the blame,
Arranging them around mine,
'Cause protection is my aim.

They lie around the margin
That hyenas will soon eat,
They taste as good as mine do
And my clutch remains complete.
My tactics are successful
For the reason that I cheat,
All's fair in evolution,
And that justifies deceit.

Halfmens

Northwards they gaze
Towards the fertile fields
They call Namibia.
This land was home until
Invaded by fierce men
Who drove them south
Across the Orange river
To this place;
Forsaken, mountain desert
Where they weep
Until the gods took pity
On their souls
And turned them into plants.
Halfmens they're called,
All leaning to the north.
Tall, spiny stems
With heads of crinkled leaves
Where nest red flowers
With yellow outer coats.
Homesick,
Forever in this barren land.

And here we empathize,
Dreaming of Bluebells
In cool English woods,
Where once we lived and loved.

The Birds of Trinidad

Tanagers and Jacobins,
Black Hawks soaring high;
Kiskadees and Mockingbirds,
Parrots flying by.

Honeycreepers, Hummingbirds,
Trogons on a branch;
Bananaquits and Flycatchers,
An avian avalanche.

Feathers scarlet, green and gold,
Wings of every size;
Bearded Bellbird, perching high,
Resonating cries.

Barn Owls floating through the air,
Nightjars on the ground;
Potoos imitating trees;
Nocturnal owlish sounds.

Cattle Egrets tiptoe through
Long, exotic grass;
Jacanas flash their yellow wings,
Vultures slowly pass.

Black Skimmers cut the surface gloss,
Ibis blush their charms;
Pelicans roost along the beach,
Toucans in the palms.

Oilbirds spend the day in caves,
Eating fruit at night;
Green tourists flock to see them there,
To everyone's delight.

White-bearded Manakins display,
Mechanically shake;
The sight and sound of these male birds
Will soon the females wake.

But will they wake the human race
Before it is too late;
Conserve the island and its birds,
Or leave them to their fate.

California Condors

The cliffs glowed vermilion;
The chances a million
To one against
Of making a sighting
Of Condors alighting
On guano splattered rocks.

A shout from our leader.
We hardly believe the
Great observation,
But floating and gliding
Two Condors arriving
Over the skyline.

Maybe they watch us,
Prudently cautious
Of human intrusion.
We honour their presence.
A treasured experience
Of hot Arizona.

Reflections

I saw shining white bark
Of the trembling aspen
Reflect in dark water
That lies in a deep lake,
Which formed from a cavern
Dissolved in the limestone
Not far from the north rim
That borders Grand Canyon.

But later in spring time
The leaves will soon flutter
On flexible leaf stalks
That christen this species.
They grow and delight us
With restless reflections
Found in the pine forests
Of hot Arizona.

Remember this image,
Diminish depression,
Reverse the dark moments
That will blight the future.
The beauty of nature
Will come to the rescue,
Give reason for living
And hope for the dying,
Escaping the torments
Of living forever.

Saguaro

Saguaro grows slow flowers show melon scented
bee contented bat frequented fruits bright scarlet ripe
contrasting sight of jet black beads birds feed scatter seeds
the young saguaro shading needs
seedlings push above the bush one foot in fifteen years
branched leafless spiny stem appears inducing fears
in herbivores with champing jaws competing for
the water store saguaro draws from desert sand
to make each pleated post expand
woodpecker bores long spines ignores to form a nest
a place of rest to rear her young amongst these giants
these cactus plants who will outlive a man.

Bryce Canyon

The sunlight enhances
Bright colour advances
Now orange in dawn light
Emerging from dark night.
These hoodoos of limestone
Maybe they are wind-blown?
But as they are rising
It's hardly surprising
The fast flowing river
Will cut ever deeper.
Their shape, rearranging
Continually changing
The view of the canyon,
Depending on season,
The light and the weather
Reacting together.
A place to remember
This day in September.

The sunlight entrances
The human mind dances
Dawn scarlet, excited
Our bodies delighted.
Here anger is unknown
Bad feelings we disown.
Our spirits uplifting
Deliciously drifting.
This view will deliver
Escape from the river
Of life, that's directing
Events. I'm expecting,
Whatever the season
Without any reason
At end of my tether,
Depression forever.
Hope helps us remember
In depths of December.

Paradise Lodge on Mount Rainier

The melting snow lasts late in paradise;
White shining Glacier Lilies grace the ice,
Pink Mountain Heather matches spreading phlox,
And Golden-mantled Squirrels sit on rocks,
Whilst Indian Paintbrush bravely counterpoints
The lustful lupins and the penstemons.
Soft sunlight warms the marmots on the slopes
Invading minds and raising human hopes,
To be recycled in the natural world
And so escape from torment after death.

The weather changes fast in Washington.
We walk in sunshine on one perfect day,
Admire the Western Pasqueflower's brief display,
And in the morning, early, end our stay,
Surrounded by grey, penetrating mist,
Which undermines belief they all exist,
Although our mountain memories persist.

What astral clock has led me to embrace
The memorable aspects of this place
All at one time, unable to explain
Why others visited in driving rain.
I never chose the time deliberately
The mysteries of chance just favoured me;
And so maybe my life has followed suit,
A pattern that I find hard to dispute.

Images of Spain

Muffled footsteps in the sand
Between the glaring white
Of pilgrims' lodgings in El Rocio.
The black Madonna of the marsh
Enthroned in splendour
In a church of gold.

The water laps around wild horses' hooves
Reflecting images of pink flamingos,
And overhead the Whiskered Terns
Are chaperoned by Collared Pratincoles.

The naked cliff provides a place for nests
Of Griffon Vultures and a coal-black Stork,
Whilst nearer, the Blue Rock Thrush rests,
And gleams his colour
Matching Spanish skies.

We watch enthralled as vultures glide
And ride the thermals
Warmed by sun-kissed rocks,
And hope to glimpse majestic, soaring birds
To satisfy our quest for Golden Eagles.

Pizarro rides above Trujillo's square,
And Incas hang emblazoned on a frieze,
Whilst we sit sampling the ice-cold beer,
And taste the time of previous centuries.

Black Jackdaws caw around the castle's towers,
And Lesser Kestrels scythe the dusty air
To feed their young beneath the bull-ring's roof.

Now the Great Bustards flaunt their bubble baths
By fluffing out the feathers of their tails,
And Little Bustards, known as farting ducks,

Inflate their necks and make the popping sound
That stimulates the females of their kind.

We climb the steps that fringe Montfrague's mound
To rest among the ruins of that place,
And listen to the calling of the Choughs
Reminding us of distant Pembroke shores,
Recalling us to end our holiday.

Gentians

What is it about a gentian
That justifies its name of king?
The richness of its regal blue
That satisfies the words that sing
Its praises.

Maybe its height above the sea,
On mountain moorland trumpeting
The brief advent of summer sun
That coaxes its brief opening
Of splendour.

But legend tells a different tale,
Of one who sent an arrow speeding
Into the heart of one such flower,
And used its root to stop his people dying
From the plague.

They punctuate the alpine grass;
Their trumpets stand, exhibiting
To bees their light interiors
With tubes of sweetness leading
To the nectar.

The courtiers come for a royal repast,
Their payment, the pollen grains they bring,
Ensuring that in years to come
The gentians are still inhabiting
Their kingdom.

Scarce Swallowtail Butterfly

Black, white, yellow and blue
Adorn the wings, on which you flew,
High on the hills in northern Spain;
You won't survive the winter rain.
Your eggs are laid on sloe; green-leaved;
When hatched, no bird will be deceived
By green, red spots and yellow stripes,
But will avoid the painful gripes,
Which might succeed a careless meal;
No need for colours that conceal.
But really it extends a gland
That best explains these coloured bands.
This gland appears behind the head
To fill the bird with startled dread.
It then emits a powerful scent
Which may reverse the bird's intent.

Cold winter brings a chrysalis
In which occurs a synthesis;
A new adult, which flies in spring
And soon is egg-depositing.
Sometimes she rests. Her wings are closed;
False markings like a head exposed;
Each tail looks like a real antenna
Just adding to a bird's dilemma.

To some you're just a butterfly;
A few brief months before you die.
Your life I wish to celebrate,
Not wanting to annihilate
Your beauty in a killing jar.
Live lovely Lepidoptera!

Chariot drawn by Doves †

This purple paradox
Brings death by doves.
My heart forgets its purpose.
The hooded monk has stolen my last breath.
My memory forgets the floral chariot.
The doves offered their nectar.
Peace at last.

† Monkshood. *Aconitum anglicum*

Memories of Iceland

Blocks of jagged lava meet us
In this land of steam and snow;
Smell of sulphur, sickly, greets us
As we touch the lava flow.

Jets of steam and boiling water
Punctuate the day-long night.
Grinding glaciers slowly falter
In the warmth of summer light.

Rivers roar past rocky ledges,
Water falls through rainbow spray;
Grasses, rushes, spiky sedges,
Moorland plants their flowers display.

Snipe above the grassland drumming,
Golden Plovers blotched with black
In their summer plumage gleaming.
Redshank calls deter attack.

Ptarmigans match the vegetation,
Falcons hunt to feed their brood,
Soaring high in desperation,
Searching for their youngster's food.

Goldeneyes catch swirling black flies,
Rising from the silent lake,
Encouraged by the warmth of sunrise.
Their larval life they must forsake.

Rafts of Eiders softly calling,
Harlequins the rapids ride,
Phalaropes catch their prey by spinning,
Whilst Puffins in their burrows hide.

The birds soon ready for departure
Leaving black, volcanic sand;
Summer's short and soon comes winter,
When darkness fills this frozen land.

Flamingos in Lesvos

Flamingos flying, flashing pink
Sieving the salt-pans they cannot drink,
Extracting from the salty water
A feast of blue-green Spirulina.

Two adult birds advance towards,
Coiling their necks like feathered cords,
Their beaks reach up and point together
Making a bond that lasts forever,

Or is it that we misinterpret
This strange, delightful bird duet.
Perhaps it really was aggression;
Two males deciding domination.

The others feed with heads inverted
Until they all were disconcerted
By keen observers watching them
Perform this dancing diadem.

The birders watch this strange behaviour
Not satisfied with twitchers' tick.
Their explanations are a failure
Though couched in wordy rhetoric.

But if we cannot find a meaning
In what we see before our eyes,
What hope have humans of revealing
The falsity of written lies.

The truth is found by observation
Not dredged from deep within a book.
We search again for adaptation,
Invent new ways with which to look.

Birthday Gift in Finland

Female mosquitoes search the wood for blood,
And drift with menace round our covered heads,
Whilst gliding soundlessly between the trees
A rare inhabitant – a Ural Owl
Observes intruders in this woodland world.

Are they a threat to its dependant chick?
A fluffy fledgling perched upon a branch
Watching nine humans walk towards its tree;
Wide-eyed and motionless it stands quite still
Knowing its parents will these men attack
And use their claws to blind those foolish souls
Who point their lenses to record this day.

A day to share with this most perfect bird;
A birthday gift to match a precious stone;
A memory to mark the passing years;
A reason to reverse the ageing fears.

Reasons for a Name

How can a name encapsulate the truth
When designated in our early youth,
Reflecting what our ancestors achieved
But not inherited when we're conceived?

Lamp is the meaning of this name in Greek.
Applied to plants it seems to be unique.
Some say the hairy leaves provide a wick,
A reason my scientific mind would pick.

But poets search for magic in the names,
Suggest the petals are red, fiery flames
Which light the hedgebank where the flowers are found,
Their floral lamps guide butterflies around.

Despite, perhaps, its Latin name explained
The puzzle of the Catchfly still remained.
Its sticky stems could hardly catch a fly
Which would some extra nitrogen supply.

The names of plants are likely to mislead
And may indeed describe some other weed.
The truth lies in the evidence observed,
It is not found within the written word.

A Meeting unfulfilled

We walked within the landscape of Provence
Searching for birds migrating from the Alps,
A visit we had planned for many years
Hoping to see an avian rarity.

We scanned the limestone cliffs for Wall Creepers
Who should have wintered on these weathered walls,
But all we saw were Jackdaws calling there
To fill our minds with memories of home.

The birds had failed to keep their rendezvous
And we were left to live our lives alone,
Forever feeling, despite azure skies,
An emptiness that we can never fill.

These are the meetings that control our lives,
Events that didn't happen in the past,
Leading to futures we did not foresee,
Controlled by probabilities of chance.

Encounter in Seychelles

Here, near an island viewpoint on Cousin,
Black frigatebirds, those pirates of the air,
Patrol the balmy currents of the sea
In which this fragment of Gondwanaland
Provides a home for White-tailed Tropicbirds.

Unknowingly we stood beside a chick
Just resting on the ground beneath a tree.
A fluffy cushion waiting to be fed.

An adult bird approached us without fear
Floating before us to distract our gaze,
Attempting to protect this fledgling bird
From tall intruders threatening its young.

I managed to record on camera
This true example of parental care,
Exhibited by parents for their young
On this secluded island in Seychelles.

Yet when I am confronted by the news,
And face the frequent stories of neglect,
I know that all the children of our kind
Deserve the love of parents who protect.
The care I witnessed of that tropicbird
Provides example for the human race.
The lack of love so often evident
In our own species, these ideals debase.

Pitcher Plant as seen by an Atheist

I taste the nectar on the glassy rim,
I slip and slide beyond the pitcher's brim,
Enzymes digest the digits of each limb,
Unable to escape, I cannot swim,
I scream, the future's fast becoming dim,
Is my existence just the futile whim
Of some vindictive God, hope's antonym?
I die, refusing to believe in Him.

The Meteor Swarm

Meteors in rapid flight,
Random dashes of delight
Stab into my mind tonight.
Poetic patterns now ignite
A streak of words in shining light,
The world appears in black and white.

Boat Orchid †

A boat sets sail along the orchid's lip
Manoeuvring between the crimson isles
On waxen water, floating through the flower
From upland forests found in far Vietnam,
To land at last within my living room.

And there they grow, most permanent of flowers,
Reflecting beauty in a woman's eyes,
Who watches them, but does not understand,
The meaning of their journey through my mind,
To flower again within her empty womb.

But mutant screams soon end the pregnant pause,
For genes will change their form haphazardly
Without regard for dreams and human hopes.
The orchid dies, its petals decompose,
The rotting body decorates the tomb.

† *Cymbidium insigne.*

Stick to your own Kind!

Peacock said to Painted Lady
"May I take you out to dine? "
He took her to the Buddleja bush,
Where they sampled nectar wine.

He tried to entertain her
By standing on his head,
When he appeared to be an owl,
Which frightened her instead.

Nearby a passing Admiral
Dressed handsomely in red,
Was asking a Small Tortoiseshell
To join him in his bed.

But females have the final choice
Of males with whom to mate,
And stick to their own species
If they wish to replicate.

Children of War

Sycamore branches, so recently refreshed with green,
Will lift the keys of chance high in the wind
That children love to hasten on their way
By throwing them with laughter in the air
To spin to some damp corner unforeseen
Where they will grow as merely dendroid weeds
Preventing other more exciting plants
From forming true succession to a wood
Of hawthorn, birch and finally to oaks
Whose acorns buried by forgetful Jays
Will germinate mosaics of lobed leaves
That flocculate dark black against the Moon.

If only children in this world of war
Could play without the fear of violent men
Who cannot understand the need to talk
And stop this fighting so a child can laugh,
Plant acorns that will grow into a wood
That hides the graves where lie the pointless dead.

Minsmere

Acrobats patrol the skies
Chasing the dashing dragonflies,
Skimming low above the water
Delicate, primeval slaughter!
The Hobbies feed upon the wing
Delighting the people watching.

Purposeful across the reeds
In which the Bittern nests and breeds,
A steady progress from the past,
But how long will this species last?
They boom their presence in the Spring
Inspiring the humans helping.

Cuckoo calling from a tree
Telling of unsolved mystery,
Bird, you will never know your young
Finding their way to fields far-flung.
Unaware of the hope you bring
To man on the planet, dying.

Marsh Harrier

Marsh Harrier rises from the dormant reeds,
Flies without effort on uplifted wings
Until she slowly sinks amongst the leaves
To rise again when caught upon the wind
That carries her aloft above the marsh,
Legs dangling beneath her feathered frame,
In silent survey of the prey she needs
To rule this land into another Spring.

And will I watch the sunlight on her head
Glint golden into yet another year,
Of watching moments that perhaps reveal
Perfection some call God.
But talons tear the living flesh,
No love is to be found.
Can such a God create this world
Where pain and fear abound?

Real Essex

Gleaming and glistening
The Golden Plovers gild the mud
With gold leaf.

Murmuring above the marsh
The Brent Geese circle
Searching for grass on which to graze.

Whistling Wigeon penetrate the morning air
Whilst melancholy Curlews cry
In the November sunlight.

A piercing winter wind ruffles the feathers
Of Black Godwits tails
As they probe for Baltic Tellins in the mud.

Grey Plovers plod in search of crabs,
Whilst watchful Redshanks scan the sky
For Peregrines.

The lazy Lapwings flapping flight
Is silhouetted black and white
Above the estuary.

Using its long, scarlet beak
In a way that is unique,
An Oystercatcher cleaves the cockles.

The busy Dunlin downward bent
Stitching the surface sediment
To feel for food.

The gaudy Shelducks feast on snails,
Which live in millions on the mud,
Devouring billions of bacteria.

The elegance of Avocets
Sweeping the shallows with their up-curved bills
Fulfils the beauty of this winter day.

We walked away along the shore
Delighted by the sights we saw
Of avian diversity.

The Visitors

Parading on the parapet
Reflecting ultraviolet
Blue Tits rotate upon the wires
Awakening their spring desires.
They chase away intruding rivals
Threatening our pair's survival.
Pecking round the nest box entrance
Calculating if the distance
Will allow their bodies access
To the safety of the darkness.
Now their nesting site is chosen
Hair and wool and feathers woven,
Thirteen days the hen-bird settles
On the eggs with red-brown freckles.
The male spends much time foraging
Responding to her fluttering
Feeds the female food she fancies
Searches bark upon the branches.
He dives into the nesting box
Safe from a passing cat or fox.
Both birds hunt eventually
Searching round their territory,
Looking for small caterpillars
Nestlings need to grow their feathers.
I wonder how long it will be
Before I hear them noisily,
Greet the adult food providers
Bringing a meal of garden spiders.

Every morning I observe
Trying one species to conserve,
I'm honoured by their presence here
Sharing my garden without fear.
I wonder if they are aware
Some other being who may care
Exists, giving that extra food

Preparing them to hatch a brood.
I wait as summer passes by
To watch the fledglings learn to fly.
The parent birds no longer visit
The baby tits have made their exit.
But wait I can see more than three
Are flitting in that elder tree.
Surely my eyes must be deceived
Too wonderful to be believed.
A fledgling flies through open door
And lands upon the hallway floor.
Flies out and rests upon the car
Calling its parents from afar.
I watch in silent admiration
Another Blue Tit generation.

Mosaic Puffball

Within the low-cut forest
Stood a beacon, milky white,
Parting the grass blades,
Expanding overnight.

Chance had prevented
Wanton feet from contact
With its unripe flesh.
I stood, admired, but did not
End its days within my basket.
Hurried on to find more wonders
In new grassy yards,
Crossing the high-speed rail-track,
Deep in thought.

A shout; a glance; two rapid steps
Beyond the probabilities of chance
That I should share those few square feet
Of land with death.

I searched afresh
For those inhabitants
Recycling the minerals of mankind.
The spores of doubt dispersing through my mind.

Marsh Frogs

Diabolic burbling,
Cataphonic gurgling.

The Marsh Frogs' ghastly serenade
With their vocal sacs displayed
Searching for the silent daughters
From the deep and muddy waters,
Who will endure the tight embrace
With the winner of the race.
Replaced by yet another male
Her struggles are of no avail,
Quite unable to escape
From this diabolic rape.

Now I have witnessed on this morning,
A female's sacrificial spawning.

Finger Tips pointing to the Moon

"Show me a rose," said the child.
Petals, sepals, stamens, styles,
Anthers, carpels, stigmas. Piles
Of parts upon the ground.
"But where is the rose?" said the child.

"Show me a rose," said the child.
Squash the anthers; pollen grains,
Observe the ovary, ovules stain,
Cells and nuclei on a slide,
"But where is the rose?" said the child.

Detergent, salt, then liquefy,
Add enzyme that will purify,
Treat with some ice-cold alcohol
And draw out from the interface
Long strands; a code in DNA.
"But where is the rose?" said the child.

A visit to the library,
Withdraw the books and we shall see
Words that encapsulate the flower.
The truth at last – *Rosa canina*!
The child sits puzzled, unimpressed.

"Where is the rose?"

Reflections at age Seventy-one

The year of truth passes
When the body becomes an embarrassment
And time is short.
Time to achieve the lost dreams
Crystallizing clearly in the morning
Before it is too late.

Explaining facts with clarity,
Give meaning to complexity,
Extend innate ability,
I seek to live in memory
Of students that I teach.

Only my words will reach the future.
My body forgotten.
The atoms that I loaned recycled,
Feeding the flowers
That filled the hedgerows of my life.
The march of molecules continues
Though my body dies.

And if there is regret
It lies in this:
I can no longer see the living world,
Explore diversity,
And marvel in its mystery unfurled.

A haikai
Life in an English Garden

A swirl of black Swifts
Screams through the evening air.
Summer surrounds me.

Searching the birch bark
Two Blue Tits probe for aphids.
The nest box beckons.

Disturbing dead leaves
I scatter the wolf spiders.
A Robin watches.

Wood Pigeon takes fright.
Between the willow branches
A clatter of wings.

Blackbird pinks loudly
Shattering the solitude.
Black cat approaches.

Lying on the lawn
The cat laps the scarlet blood
Amongst the feathers.

Black Crow flies above
Shadowing the chamomile.
Death roosts in my mind.

A haikai
Eight Aspects of Life

The words fall freely
Into place upon the page.
The Nightingale sings.

Roman aqueduct
Blue and gold in evening light.
Rock Sparrows roosting.

The scent of Bluebells
Buds bursting on the oak trees.
A kiss in springtime.

Safe from the Buzzards
The Rabbits leave their burrows.
The Eagle Owl wakes.

Flamingos flying
Flashing pink in the sunshine.
Can they see my tears?

Sparrowhawk sweeping
Fast and low along the ditch.
A storm of feathers.

Winter fills the air.
Murmuring above the mud
The Brent Geese circle.

Endless corridor
Stretching in both directions.
Which way did I come?

A haikai
Memories in Colour

The roan chestnuts
Lie gleaming in the litter
Of my memories.

Sky blue and silver
Camouflages the morning
Preparing for war.

Scarlet patched with white.
Promise of oblivion
Beneath the birch trees.

A tropical night
Brilliant black with silver stars
Guiding our footsteps.

Clouds grey and golden
Crowning princely podocarps.
The Kokako calls.

Firing the landscape
Orange daisies kiss the sun.
Tears moisten my eyes.

In mountain grassland
Royal gentians reflect
The colour of kings.

Limestone glows golden.
Ascending through the shadows
The hoodoos worship.

Many shades of green
Spring's palette paints the woodlands.
I long for England.

Forgotten Sense

Walking the corridors around the wards
When visiting the woman that I loved,
A sweet-sick scent diffused into my mind –
As if a bullet had this moment struck my heart.
Suddenly, I was back in college labs
Anaesthetizing fruit flies in a tube,
The smell of ether unforgettable.
Or in a factory another smell
Took me again to making many slides
To see the details of the chromosomes
Squashed from the anthers of a purple flower
And treated with the pungent oil of cloves.
A memory brought forth so vividly
That I recalled another striking smell;
The stink of rotten eggs took me at once
To dingy school labs where analysis
Required the use of this obnoxious gas
Which bubbled through the test-tube fricassee
Identified the metals in the broth.
And then I was transported to long hours
Dissecting dogfish in another lab
Foul formalin spiced up with piscine stench
That I could never possibly forget.
But oh the scent of Bluebells in the wood
Where hands were held and I first kissed your lips;
Pleasure forever etched upon my mind.

Heliconia

A gold and scarlet passion
Is burning in the shadows
Of Eve's botanic garden.
Alone, we can imagine
The humming birds that hover,
Search, and then discover
The sweetness of the nectar.
But could we come together
At a meeting in midsummer
When both of us remember,
As Lyra did before us,
The magic of those moments
In another universe.

The Fall of the Ideal

Tormented shadows of the night,
Those gnarled shapes twisting skywards,
Yet I have seen much taller trees
Collapse, and die like cowards.

Anemones now grace the woods
With starry, white corollas,
Yet I have seen much prettier flowers
Fall back beneath the stars.

Perfection lies within the mind,
Continually projected;
Yet, when it falls upon the earth,
Its patterns are rejected.

Night on the Norfolk Broads

That night I was free
Under the canopy
Of stars.
Shadows danced along the furrows,
Raced across the open meadows,
Tripped, and fell among the burrows
On the bank.
Along the shadow of the lane,
Another shadow practically insane
Whirls and leaps and somersaults
Over the hedges lightly vaults,
Whilst I remain,
Sleepless for thirty-six hours,
Intoxicated by the moonlit landscape.

Cautionary Tale

Tarantula hides in the toilet.
Beth enters the bathroom en suite.
The full Moon rose early this morning
As Beth made a dash for the street.

She quickly regained her composure
And beat a strategic retreat.
Now each time she visits the bathroom
She always looks under the seat.

Thoughts
(on observing my toes in the bath)

Pneumatophores
On mangrove shores
My toes emerged
From legs submerged.
I contemplate
The human state,
But mind disowns
These ageing bones.
Where to reside
When I have died?
Escape my flesh
And start afresh.
Could I but grow
An embryo,
Where I could live,
A fugitive
From certain death.

Natural Selection

A halophyte called Scurvy Grass
Invades the verge along the pass,
Whilst galaxies of Queen Anne's Lace
Are colonizing roadside space.

But Venus's Chariot drawn by Doves
A wetland habitat this plant loves
Competing with Policeman's Helmet
Which easily will soon outgrow it.

Lords and Ladies grow in shade
Burst forth red berries when they fade,
Surviving deep within dark woods
Yet dying in bright neighbourhoods.

These plants appear to be designed,
Their form and features so aligned,
As if a God seemed to invent
A match for each environment.

Chance produces variations
Some of them are adaptations
Which survive and are selected...
Apparently as if created.

Why not Eleonora's Orchid?

The princess called Eleonora
Had no love at all for the flora.
When it came to the falcon
Her name quickly caught on,
But only the birders adore her.

Penduline Tits

What is it that is watching me
From deep within the mystery
Amongst the reed stems opposite?
They just appeared quite suddenly,
Four members of a family
Of tiny birds that we call tits.
Described by man as penduline
Whose nest's a marvel of design,
That all their predators outwits.
These birds show curiosity;
No sign of animosity.
In what way could they benefit?
Our lives are firmly intertwined
And love is all that I can find.
A meeting with the infinite.

Walking through Life with Judith

For you are not a chain around my neck
Preventing my escape into the light.
Instead you are a lifebelt 'round my waist
That stops me sinking slowly out of sight.
So do not walk alone to meet your God
Leaving me lonely in an alien world,
But let us walk together through the night
To face as one the stones that fate has hurled.

Enlightenment

I clearly see the reason now
The reason for my malady,
The missing mentor to inspire
And motivate my history.
No father, lover, friend or god
Gave insight to my destiny,
And so I chose to avoid change,
A teacher of biology.
My students satisfy their needs
And enter university,
My words reach to the future, far,
Into the world of mystery,
My DNA has recombined
And colonised new territory,
But when I die, my life complete,
Without the need of sympathy,
Recycled in the natural world
Surviving in life's poetry.

Glossary of words and phrases

Antennae

A pair of appendages called feelers on the head of an insect.

Antonym

A word opposite in meaning to another.

Altruism in the Natural World

Living and acting for the benefit of others. It usually applies to related individuals.

Baltic Tellins

Bivalve molluscs or shellfish with two very long siphons.

Banksias

Woody plants of the family Proteaceae, which grow in Australia. They were once called native honeysuckles as they attract nectar-feeding birds.

Booyong tree

Tall trees, which grow in Queensland's rainforest and have strongly buttressed trunks at their bases. The scientific name is *Heritiera trifoliata*

Buddleja

A flowering plant called the Butterfly Bush, *Buddleja davidii*, which is attractive to butterflies that feed on the nectar it produces.

Cataphonics

The science of echoes or reflected sounds.

Catchfly

A plant called Sticky Catchfly, *Lychnis viscaria,* seen in Finland.

Chamomile

A plant, *Chamaemelum nobile,* that can be used to make a lawn, although it does not stand up to heavy wear.

Chariot drawn by Doves

A local name for the plant Monkshood, *Aconitum anglicum.*

Chrysalis
A stage in the life cycle of many insects. Inside this pupa the tissues of the larva or caterpillar are reorganized to form the body of the adult insect.

Collared Pratincole
A species of wading bird, *Glareola pratincola.*

Corollas
The collective name for all the petals of a flower.

Dendroid
A word that means tree-like.

Diadem
A jewelled headband or crown.

DNA
The chemical deoxyribonucleic acid that genes are made of.

Ecosystem
The result of an interaction between a community of organisms and their non-living environment e.g. a tropical rain forest.

El Rocio
A town on the edge of the Donana National Park in Andalucia in Spain.

Enzyme
A protein that will speed up a specific chemical reaction, but which remains unchanged at the end.

Escaping the torments of living forever
A reference to Philip Pullman's trilogy of novels called 'His Dark Materials'.

Fingertips pointing to the Moon
A phrase originating in Zen Buddhism meaning that all instruction is but a finger pointing to the Moon, and that those whose gaze is fixed upon the pointer will never see beyond.

Fiordland
This region occupies ten percent of New Zealand's land area and includes a large National Park.

Flame trees

These trees are covered in brilliant, red flowers in Spring before the leaves develop. The scientific name is *Brachychiton populneus.* They grow in Queensland and New South Wales.

Fruit flies

Insects in the genus *Drosophila* used in genetic experiments.

Guano

The droppings of birds leaving white deposits on rocks, which can be used as a source of phosphate fertilizer.

Gondwanaland

The great southern continent, which gave rise to the present day continents by the process of plate tectonics, which replaced the older theory of continental drift.

Haikai

A group of several related haikus. A haiku is a verse form, which consists of three lines with five, seven and five syllables respectively.

Halfmens

Remarkable plants called *Pachypodium namaquanum*, which we saw in the Goegap Nature Reserve during our trip to Namaqualand, South Africa.

Halophyte

A plant that can grow in very salty conditions e.g. Danish Scurvy Grass, *Cochlearia danica.* It is spreading along the verges of the main roads from the coast of Essex because of the salt used to prevent ice formation.

Heliconia

Plants native to tropical America, which are pollinated by humming birds. The one in my poem was growing in a glasshouse in the Oxford Botanic Garden.

Hoodoos

Large rock pinnacles cut by water erosion that are found in Bryce Canyon in Utah, USA.

Kokako

A New Zealand species of native perching birds (Passerines), which lives in podocarp forests and has a song consisting of a slow string of very loud, rich, mournful, organ-like notes.

Kookaburra

A large kingfisher, which feeds on insects and small vertebrates but not fish. They have a characteristic laughing call.

Lepidoptera

The order of insects to which the butterflies and moths belong.

Lesvos

A Greek island formerly called Lesbos.

Lyra

The second Eve, who is the young heroine in Philip Pullman's trilogy of novels called 'His Dark Materials'. She has many adventures and eventually releases the souls of the dead from perpetual torment to be recycled in the natural world.

Lords-and-Ladies

Arum maculatum, which has more common names than any other British plant.

Megapodes

Birds related to pheasants, which scratch and pile sand, soil and vegetation litter into a large mound. The male builds the mound and the female then lays her eggs in it where they are kept warm by the sun and by the heat generated by the decaying litter.

Meteors

Shooting stars produced when particles of rock or dust burn up in the Earth's atmosphere. We saw many of them from our coach on the way to the airport in Israel.

Monogamy

The condition of having one mate at a time.

Montfrague's mound

The site of a ruined castle in Spain.

Mosaic Puffball

The fruiting body of a fungus, *Handkea utriformis*, which is spherical with a short, broad stalk. The developing spores are completely enclosed until it is ripe.

Mutant

An organism formed as the result of a spontaneous change in a gene or in the form or number of a chromosome.

Nebulae

These are clouds of interstellar gas and dust some types of which glow.

Paradise Lodge

A hotel in Washington State, USA

Penduline Tits

Birds seen in Bulgaria whose complex nest hangs over water from a branch to avoid predators.

Pitcher plant

An insectivorous plant, *Nepenthes pervillei.* The one we saw in the wild was growing in the Seychelles.

Pneumatophores

Aerial roots of plants like mangroves, which stick up above the waterlogged mud and obtain oxygen for the plant.

Podocarps

Very impressive cone bearing trees, which we saw in New Zealand, including a very tall species *Podocarpus dacrydioides*. It is also called White Pine or the Fruit Basket of the Forest.

Policeman's Helmet

Himalayan Balsam, *Impatiens glandulifera,* which is colonising river banks in Britain. It has fruits, which explode when ripe.

Provence

An area of France.

Queen Anne's Lace

Cow Parsley, *Anthriscus sylvestris,* which is becoming dominant on roadside verges as it can survive being cut down regularly.

Rosa canina
The scientific name for the dog rose.

Saguaro
This plant is the very famous giant cactus called *Carnegiea giganteus*. Its blossom is the state flower of Arizona.

Spirulina
This microbe was once thought to be a blue-green alga, but is now known to be a bacterium. It is used in health foods and smoothies.

Succession
The sequence of communities that colonise bare rock, soil or open water until a climax community is reached e.g. grassland, then scrub and finally woodland.

Takahe
A large, rare, flightless bird introduced into Tiritiri Matangi. It is related to swamphens and coots. The individual described in my poem is now unfortunately dead having had to be put down after damaging one of its legs. It was a great attraction for bird-watchers before its demise.

Tarantula
A very large spider, which we saw on the wall in a restaurant in Trinidad. Later it inspired my poem Cautionary Tale.

Tiritiri Matangi
The name of a small island off the coast of the North Island of New Zealand.

Trujillo
A town in Extremadura in Spain. It was the birthplace of Pizarro, the conquistador who conquered Peru and killed many of the Incas, who lived there.

Wandering Albatross
A sea-bird with the longest wingspan of any bird up to 3.4 meters.

Other natural history poetry books by Brambleby Books

Fascinating Felines – 60 cat poems
Hugh D. Loxdale, ISBN 9780954334703

The Eternal Quest – Celebration of Nature in Poetry
Hugh D. Loxdale, ISBN 9780954334710

Blue Skies in Tuscany – Poems about Life, Love…and Lesser Burdock
Hugh D. Loxdale, ISBN 9780954334727

Bird Words – Poetic Images of Wild birds
Hugh D. Loxdale, ISBN 9780954334734

Up High and Invisible
Keith Davies, ISBN 9780954334758

One under the Sun – A collection of poems
Vincent Spada, ISBN 9780955392863

Love and the Sea
Hugh D. Loxdale, ISBN 9780955392887

The Jena Poems
Hugh D. Loxdale, ISBN 9780955392894

Nevisian Days – Poetry from a Caribbean Isle
Hugh D. Loxdale, ISBN 9781908241009

Bird of Paradise – Selected poems, 1968-2011
Hugh D. Loxdale, ISBN 9781908241016

www.bramblebybooks.co.uk

Follow us on Facebook!